the Sheldon Harnick SONGBOOK

Cover photo by Margery Gray Harnick

ISBN 978-1-4234-2258-7

WILLIAMSON MUSIC®
A RODGERS AND HAMMERSTEIN COMPANY
www.williamsonmusic.com

EXCLUSIVELY DISTRIBUTED BY

HAL•LEONARD® CORPORATION
7777 W. BLUEMOUND RD. P.O. BOX 13819 MILWAUKEE, WI 53213

Visit Hal Leonard Online at
www.halleonard.com

SHELDON HARNICK

Introduction

Of the 33 songs in this book, all but two are from musicals (stage or television) and musical revues. Although two were originally written for cabaret performers and three were written simply to explore amusing notions that popped into my head, it says something about the inherent theatricality of these five songs that they all wound up in musical revues. [The remaining two songs were written as themes for films.]

As a writer, what whets my appetite (and, on occasion, unnerves me) is the challenge of writing for a specific character in a specific situation in a specific time and place. This approach, of course, considerably narrows the number of songs that can be fully effective when performed out of context. But, for me, that has always been a secondary consideration. What is important to me is to have a character come fully live onstage, giving vent to his or her emotions in a way that is credible, comprehensible and meaningful to an audience. I want that audience to be entertained but I also want that audience to believe the character who's singing and, ideally, to identify with the thoughts and feelings being expressed.

Most of these songs are the fruits of a life spent in the musical theatre. My lyrical heroes are all writers who have written extensively for the theatre: W.S. Gilbert, E.Y. Harburg, Irving Berlin, Lorenz Hart, Oscar Hammerstein, Frank Loesser, Stephen Sondheim—the list goes on and on. Like them (and, no doubt, *because* of them) I have tried to create lyrics that are fresh, truthful and unpredictable, while remaining fluid and conversational. The theatre has given me more than my share of joy and pain—more of the former, I'm happy to say, than the latter. And, along the way, it has provided me with my favorite phrase in the English language: "We're in rehearsal."

Sheldon Harnick
New York City
June, 2007

SHELDON HARNICK

Born April 30, 1924 and raised in Chicago, Sheldon Harnick began studying the violin while in grammar school. After serving in the U.S. Army for three years, he enrolled in the Northwestern University School of Music, and earned a Bachelor of Music degree in 1949. Though his focus had been the violin, Harnick also developed skills as a writer of comedy sketches, songs and parody lyrics, and eventually decided to try his luck as a theatrical lyricist in New York City.

His first song in a Broadway show, "The Boston Beguine" for *New Faces of 1952*, introduced theatergoers to the wry, subtle humor and deft wordplay indicative of a Harnick lyric. Over the next several years he contributed lyrics or whole songs to such vintage revues as *John Murray Anderson's Almanac*, *The Shoestring Revue* and *The Littlest Revue*.

A few more years were spent working on other writers' trouble-plagued Broadway-bound musicals before Harnick joined up with composer Jerry Bock to write their own musicals. While the first Bock & Harnick musical, *The Body Beautiful* (1958) showed promise, it was their second musical, *Fiorello!* (1959), that put the team on the map. Their musical biography of New York City's legendary mayor earned the Tony® Award, Pulitzer Prize and New York Drama Critics' Circle Award. Their next musical, *Tenderloin* (1960), set in the seamy Tenderloin district of late 19th century New York, was followed by *She Loves Me* (1963), which beguiled audiences with its Central European charm and operatic elegance.

In 1964, Bock & Harnick, working with director-choreographer Jerome Robbins and book writer Joseph Stein, created a musical masterpiece that vividly evoked a vanished community while telling a story with universal and timeless appeal. *Fiddler on the Roof*, based on a series of short stories by Jewish folklorist Sholom Alecheim, earned the Tony® Award, New York Drama Critics' Circle Award, a gold record (for both its Broadway cast album and film soundtrack recordings) and a platinum record (for the Broadway album.) In 1971, with the Broadway production still running, United Artists released the film version starring Topol. The following year the stage production became the longest-running show in Broadway history, a record it held until 1979.

After *Fiddler*, the Bock & Harnick collaboration went on to include such versatile fare as *The Apple Tree* (1966), which was comprised of three one-act musicals, and *The Rothschilds* (1970), an epic telling of the founding of the Rothschild banking dynasty.

Harnick's other collaborators in musical theatre have included: Michel Legrand, for whom Harnick translated *The Umbrellas of Cherbourg* (1979) before working together on a musical of *A Christmas Carol* (1981); Mary Rodgers, with whom Harnick wrote a version of *Pinocchio* (1973) for the famed Bil Baird Marionettes, and a song, "William's Doll," for Marlo Thomas' *Free to Be...You and Me* (1974); Richard Rodgers, joining forces for the score to *Rex* (1976), a Broadway musical about Henry VIII; Joe Raposo, where their joint credits included *Sutter's Gold* (1980), a cantata premiered by the Boston Symphony Orchestra, and *A Wonderful Life* (1986), a musical based on Frank Capra's holiday classic; and Arnold Black, with whom he created a musical version of Norton Juster's popular children's book, *The Phantom Tollbooth* (2002), in collaboration with Mr. Juster. A solo work, *Dragons* (1984), was based on a Russian play and given its premiere at Harnick's alma mater, Northwestern University.

Harnick has provided English-language librettos for classical operas and oratorios, including works by Stravinsky, Ravel, Mozart, Bach and Verdi. His version of Lehar's *The Merry Widow* (1977) was premiered by the San Diego Opera Company starring Beverly Sills (a subsequent album won the 1979 GRAMMY Award® for best new opera recording). His translation of Georges Bizet's *Carmen* was commissioned and premiered by the Houston Grand Opera (1981) and served as the English text for Peter Brooks' acclaimed *La Tragedie de Carmen* (1984). His translations of several Yiddish songs were featured in the Los Angeles and New York productions of Joshua Sobol's play *Ghetto* (1986), and he collaborated on the English libretto for the Broadway production of the Dutch musical *Cyrano* (1993). His original opera librettos include *Doctor Heidegger's Fountain of Youth* (1978), music by Jack Beeson; *Love in Two Countries* (1991), music by Thomas Z. Shepard; and *Coyote Tales* (1998), music by Henry Mollicone, based on Native American trickster tales.

His work for television and film ranges from songs for the HBO animated film, *The Tale of Peter Rabbit* (1991) with music by Stephen Lawrence, to lyrics for the opening number of the 1988 Academy Awards telecast. He wrote the theme songs for two films, both with music by Cy Coleman: *The Heartbreak Kid* (1972) and *Blame It on Rio* (1984).

Sheldon Harnick is a member of The Dramatists Guild and the Songwriters Guild of America. In addition to his Tonys®, Pulitzer and GRAMMYs®, his many other honors include: The Johnny Mercer Award presented by the Songwriters Hall of Fame; the Marc Blitzstein Memorial Award for achievement in the creation of opera librettos, presented by the American Academy and Institute of Arts and Letters; and an Honorary Doctorate of Humane Letters awarded by Illinois Wesleyan University and Muskingum College. In 2005, he and his wife, Margery, celebrated their fortieth anniversary with their children Beth and Matthew.

On Working in the Theatre
(for Burton Lane)

Knowing of the sniper,
nevertheless I stood,
waved my arms,
sang, danced,
smiled.

In bright light,
naked and afraid,
I stood
knowing of the waiting gun.

Surprised and not surprised,
wounded, I fell,
bled, sighed,
died.

What was most meaningful
to do,
I did.
What else could I have done?

Sheldon Harnick
4/12/79

IS THIS THE LITTLE GIRL I CARRIED
  "   "   "   BOY AT PLAY
I DON'T REMEMBER GROWING OLDER
WHEN DID THEY?
WHEN DID SHE GET TO BE A BEAUTY
  "   "   HE GROW " " SO TALL
WASN'T IT YESTERDAY WHEN THEY WERE SMALL—

SUNRISE, SUNSET
   "   "
SWIFTLY FLOW THE DAYS
SEEDLINGS TURN OVERNIGHT TO SUNFLOWERS
BLOSSOMING EVEN AS WE GAZE

SUNRISE, SUNSET
   "   "
SWIFTLY FLY THE YEARS
ONE SEASON FOLLOWING ANOTHER
LADEN WITH HAPPINESS AND TEARS—

NOW IS THE LITTLE BOY A BRIDEGROOM
  "   "   "   "   GIRL " BRIDE
UNDER THE CANOPY I SEE THEM
SIDE BY SIDE—

PLACE THE GOLD RING UPON HER FINGER
SHARE THE { ~~SWEET~~ } WINE AND BREAK THE GLASS
SOON THE FULL CIRCLE WILL HAVE COME TO PASS—

SUNRISE, SUNSET — etc.

Original draft of the lyrics for "Sunrise, Sunset" from *Fiddler on the Roof*.
Courtesy of the New York Public Library for the Performing Arts,
Music Division, the Sheldon Harnick Collection.

Photo: Nicholas Rhodes

1959 The *Fiorello!* team:
George Abbott,
Jerome Weidman,
Bobby Griffith,
Hal Prince, me,
Jerry Bock at piano

1963 Playing the score of *She Loves Me*
for Barbara Cook and Hal Prince;
me singing, Jerry Bock playing

1965 *Fiddler on the Roof* wins the Drama
Critics' Circle Award (l. to r.): Harold Prince,
Jerome Robbins, Jerry Bock, me,
Joe Stein and Ted Kalem

STUDIO
COLUMNBIA
RECORDS

1966 *The Apple Tree*
recording session, with Jerry Bock

Photo: David Gahr

9

1966 The Apple Tree
recording session,
with Barbara Harris
and Jerry Bock

Photo: David Gahr

1976 *Rex* recording session:
listening with Co-Producer Roger Berlind

Photo: Margery Gray Harnick

1976 *Rex* recording session: with conductor
Jay Blackton and Producer Thomas Shepard

Photo: Margery Gray Harnick

1970 With Jerry Bock
on the set of *The Rothschilds*

Photo: Martha Swope

1976 Start of rehearsals for *Rex*; Richard Rodgers at piano,
with Nicol Williamson, Penny Fuller and me

1982 At Serendipity with
son Matthew and daughter Beth

Photo: Margery Gray Harnick

1971 Performing at
"Lyrics & Lyricists" Series;
Mary Louise looks on

1985 In Paris with
son Matthew and Michel Legrand

Photo: Margery Gray Harnick

CONTENTS

1979 Performing
(location unknown)

Photo: David Stollak

ARTIFICIAL FLOWERS
from TENDERLOIN

Music by JERRY BOCK
Lyrics by SHELDON HARNICK

* pronounced like "wine"

AWAY FROM YOU
from REX

Lyrics by SHELDON HARNICK
Music by RICHARD RODGERS

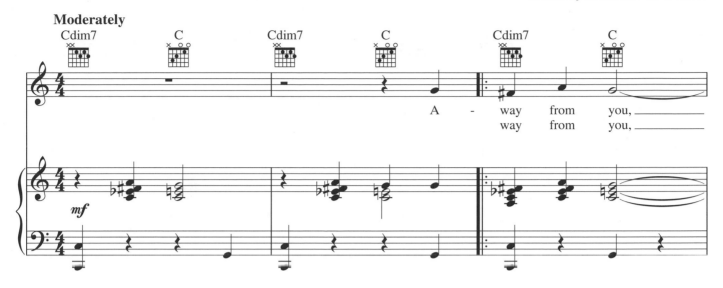

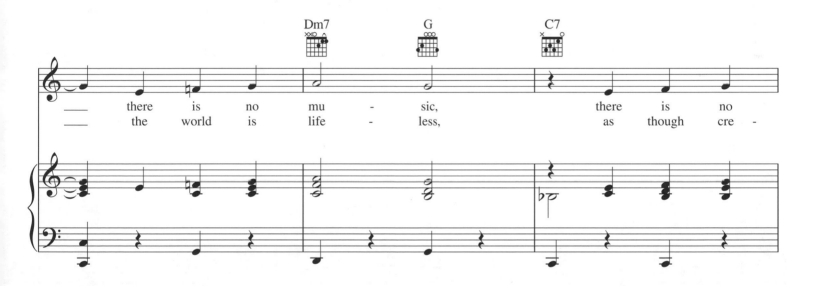

THE BALLAD OF
THE SHAPE OF THINGS
from THE LITTLEST REVUE

Words and Music by
SHELDON HARNICK

*To rhyme with "far"

BLAME IT ON RIO
from the Film BLAME IT ON RIO

Music by CY COLEMAN
Lyrics by SHELDON HARNICK

THE BOSTON BEGUINE

from Leonard Sillman's NEW FACES OF 1952

Words and Music by
SHELDON HARNICK

*For Boy: Softly I whispered to her,

Coda

moon_____ We fell a - sleep in Bos - ton._____ That was the sto - ry_____ of my one ro-mance there!_____ Our dream of ad - ven - ture_____ did-n't stand a chance there!_____ How could we hope to en - joy_____ all the plea - sures a - head_____ When the books we should have read_____

CHRISTMAS GIFTS

from A WONDERFUL LIFE

Music by JOE RAPOSO
Lyrics by SHELDON HARNICK

I COULDN'T BE WITH ANYONE BUT YOU

from A WONDERFUL LIFE

Music by JOE RAPOSO
Lyrics by SHELDON HARNICK

EVERLASTING LIGHT
(A Song for Chanukah)

Words by SHELDON HARNICK
Music by DAVID SHIRE

Moderato, steadily

Flames of free-dom, _____ may we live to see your brief can-dles _____ burn e-ter-nal-ly, bless-ing us with _____ Ev-er-last-ing Light. _____

IF I WERE A RICH MAN
from the Musical FIDDLER ON THE ROOF

Words by SHELDON HARNICK
Music by JERRY BOCK

Freely

Boi, boi, boi, boi, boi, boi, boi, boi, boi. __

Deliberately (in tempo)

And it won't make one bit of dif - f'rence

if I an - swer right or wrong.

When you're rich, they think you real - ly

Reflective

know.

If I were rich, I'd have the time that I lack to

sit in the syn - a - gogue and pray; and may - be have a seat by the east - ern

ISM
from VINTAGE '60
Dedicated to the memory of Marcia Brushingham

Words by SHELDON HARNICK
Music by DAVID BAKER

Optional: Insert monologue here.

Monologue

At least a prism is a ism I can hold in my hand. Those other isms – like anarchism – collectivism – individualism – are to me nothing but big words. And I don't understand big words. My daddy likes to use big words. He likes to indulge in flights into the rarified atmosphere of abstruse political hypothesis. And as far as I'm concerned, flights into the rarified atmosphere is for the birds. But then I'm only six – and that's a very cynical age.

Maybe I'll understand about the isms when I'm old enough to read. But my daddy talks all the time and he never reads nothing. I asked him why and he said that books made him think. And thinking unsettled his prejudices. Then he hit me. I'll bet at this very minute he's talking about isms in spasms – of cynicism – criticism – and pessimism. My daddy's a Congressman. My mommy wears earplugs.

(Back to song, at D.S.)
All the other isms
Can lead to tomfool'ry, *etc.*

IN MY OWN LIFETIME
from THE ROTHSCHILDS

Lyrics by SHELDON HARNICK
Music by JERRY BOCK

JUST A MAP
Written for THE ROTHSCHILDS

Lyrics by SHELDON HARNICK
Music by JERRY BOCK

MATCHMAKER
from the Musical FIDDLER ON THE ROOF

Words by SHELDON HARNICK
Music by JERRY BOCK

LITTLE TIN BOX
from the Musical FIORELLO!

Words by SHELDON HARNICK
Music by JERRY BOCK

MERRY LITTLE MINUET

from JOHN MURRAY ANDERSON'S ALMANAC

Words and Music by
SHELDON HARNICK

Cheerfully, crisply

They're ri-ot-ing in Af-ri-ca.
far a-way Si - be-ri-a,
(whistle... ...)
They're they

starv-ing in Spain.
freeze by the score.
(whistle... ...)
There's hur-ri-canes in Flor-i-da
An av-a-lanche in Switz-er-land

To Coda

(whistle... ...) and Tex-as needs rain.
just got fif-teen more.
(whistle... ...)
The But

whole world is fes-ter-ing with un-hap-py souls. The French hate the

82

OH, TO BE A MOVIE STAR

from THE APPLE TREE

Words and Music by JERRY BOCK
and SHELDON HARNICK

ONE FAMILY
from A CHRISTMAS CAROL

Words by SHELDON HARNICK
Music by MICHEL LEGRAND

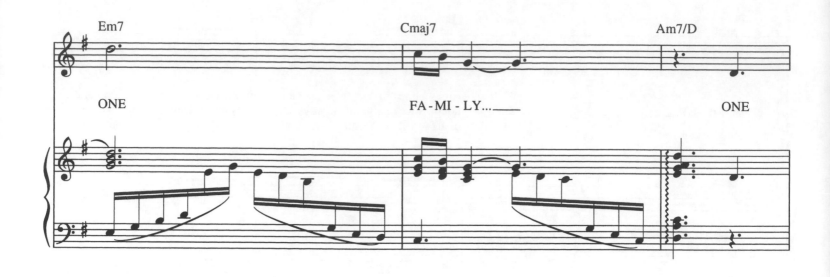

ONE   FA - MI - LY..._____   ONE

FA - MI - LY._____ _____   2.We're   4.We're

3.Since

all   of   us   tru - ly   the   chil - dren of   God.   We're leaves   in   one   book,   we're

peas in one pod. We're drops in one riv - er, we're limbs of one tree, cre -

a - ted to be ONE FA-MI-LY.... ONE

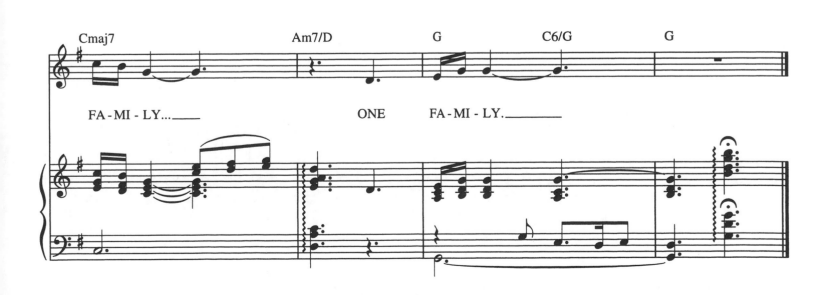

FA - MI - LY.... ONE FA - MI - LY.

PENNY BY PENNY
from A CHRISTMAS CAROL

Lyrics by SHELDON HARNICK
Music by MICHEL LEGRAND

Belle: PEN - NY   BY   PEN - NY   and day by day,

slow - ly but sure - ly we're mak - ing our way. No

tear - drops,____ no com - plaints... *Young Scrooge:* Well, there may be com -
(2.) win - ter____ leads to spring and as day fol - lows

plaints and some tears through the years, for
night, so the fu - ture must bring our

we're not plas - ter saints. *Belle:* Ho - ur by ho - ur,
share of warmth and light. Slow - ly but sure - ly,

THE PICTURE OF HAPPINESS

from TENDERLOIN

Music by JERRY BOCK
Lyrics by SHELDON HARNICK

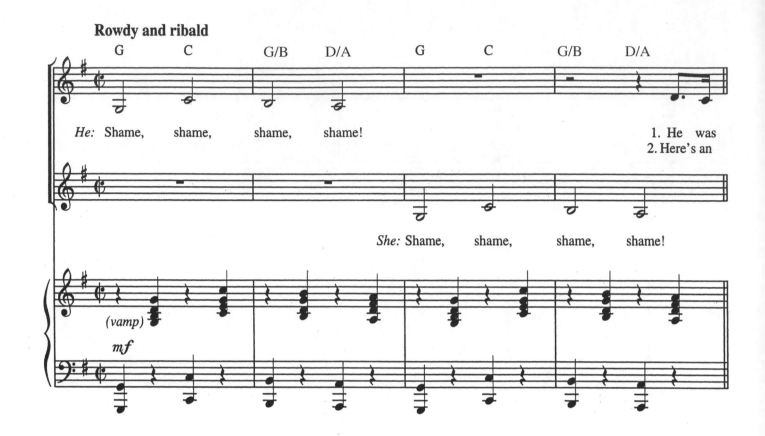

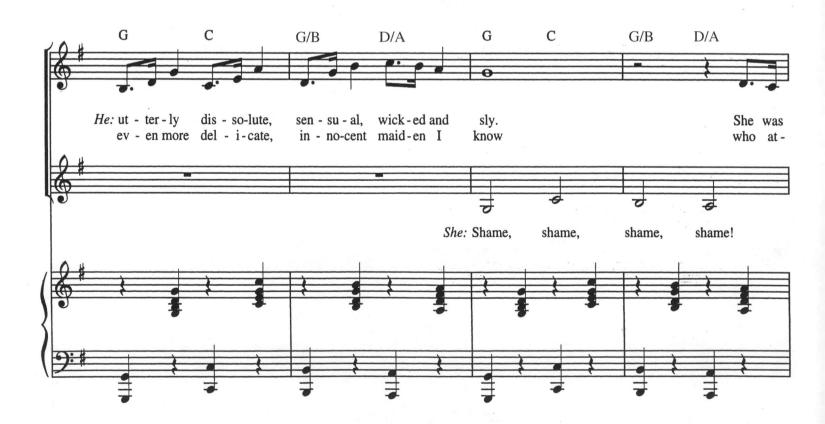

SHE LOVES ME

from SHE LOVES ME

Words by SHELDON HARNICK
Music by JERRY BOCK

SOMEONE'S BEEN SENDING ME FLOWERS

from THE SHOESTRING REVUE

Words by SHELDON HARNICK
Music by DAVID BAKER

THAT KIND OF A DAY
from the HBO TV Special THE TALE OF PETER RABBIT

Words and Music by SHELDON HARNICK
and STEPHEN LAWRENCE

SUMMER IS
from THE BODY BEAUTIFUL

Words by SHELDON HARNICK
Music by JERRY BOCK

SUNRISE, SUNSET
from the Musical FIDDLER ON THE ROOF

Words by SHELDON HARNICK
Music by JERRY BOCK

TAKE CARE OF ONE ANOTHER

from DRAGONS

Words and Music by
SHELDON HARNICK

1. This world too oft-en seems a jun-gle.... look a-
(2.)world too oft-en seems a des-ert:__ bleak and

round... look a-round... a world where we shrink from ev-'ry
bare, harsh and dry, a world where we drift in i-so-

shad-ow and we jump at ev-'ry sud-den sound. This
la-tion and our hopes too quick-ly wilt and die. This

(1st x short) rit.

'TIL TOMORROW
from the Musical FIORELLO!

Words by SHELDON HARNICK
Music by JERRY BOCK

TONIGHT AT EIGHT

from SHE LOVES ME

Words by SHELDON HARNICK
Music by JERRY BOCK

TRUE LOVE AND BEAUTIFUL MUSIC

from THE AUDITION

Music by MARVIN HAMLISCH
Lyrics by SHELDON HARNICK

Warmly, not too slowly

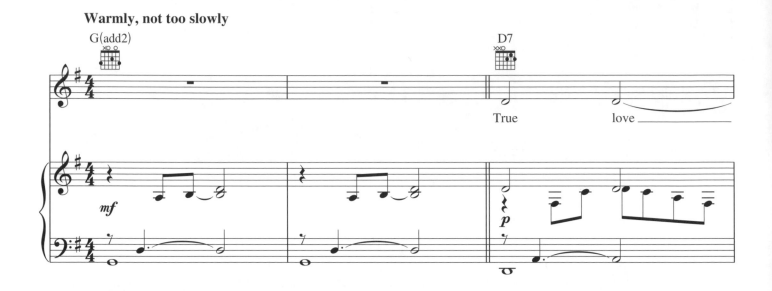

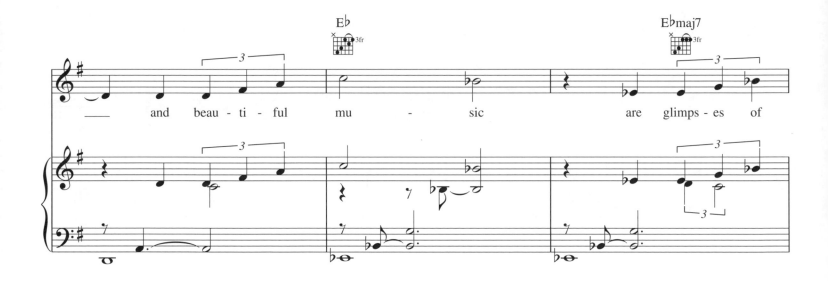

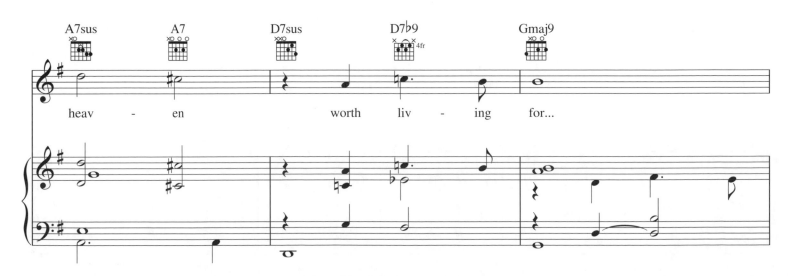

VANILLA ICE CREAM
from SHE LOVES ME

Words by SHELDON HARNICK
Music by JERRY BOCK

WHERE DO I GO FROM HERE

from the Musical FIORELLO!

Words by SHELDON HARNICK
Music by JERRY BOCK

WHEN MESSIAH COMES

Written for FIDDLER ON THE ROOF

Words by SHELDON HARNICK
Music by JERRY BOCK

YOU MADE MY DAY

from the Illustrated Collection THANKS & GIVING ALL YEAR LONG by Marlo Thomas

Words and Music by
SHELDON HARNICK

glows like a lamp in a

blue vel - vet sky.

D.C. al Coda

Broadly

CODA

You made my day." _____

YOU'RE GOING FAR
(Theme from "The Heartbreak Kid")
from the Film THE HEARTBREAK KID

Music by CY COLEMAN
Lyrics by SHELDON HARNICK